A Boy's Will

A Boy's Will

Robert Frost

MINT EDITIONS

A Boy's Will was first published in 1913.

This edition published by Mint Editions 2020.

ISBN 9781513270906 | E-ISBN 9781513275901

Published by Mint Editions®

**MINT
EDITIONS**

minteditionbooks.com

Publishing Director: Jennifer Newens
Design & Production: Rachel Lopez Metzger
Project Manager: Micaela Clark
Typesetting: Westchester Publishing Services

Contents

PART II

Part III

PART I

INTO MY OWN

One of my wishes is that those dark trees,
So old and firm they scarcely show the breeze,
Were not, as 'twere, the merest mask of gloom,
But stretched away unto the edge of doom.
I should not be withheld but that some day
Into their vastness I should steal away,
Fearless of ever finding open land,
Or highway where the slow wheel pours the sand.
I do not see why I should e'er turn back,
Or those should not set forth upon my track
To overtake me, who should miss me here
And long to know if still I held them dear.
They would not find me changed from him they knew—
Only more sure of all I thought was true.

GHOST HOUSE

I dwell in a lonely house I know
That vanished many a summer ago,
And left no trace but the cellar walls,
And a cellar in which the daylight falls,
And the purple-stemmed wild raspberries grow.
O'er ruined fences the grape-vines shield
The woods come back to the mowing field;
The orchard tree has grown one copse
Of new wood and old where the woodpecker chops;
The footpath down to the well is healed.
I dwell with a strangely aching heart
In that vanished abode there far apart
On that disused and forgotten road
That has no dust-bath now for the toad.
Night comes; the black bats tumble and dart;
The whippoorwill is coming to shout
And hush and cluck and flutter about:
I hear him begin far enough away
Full many a time to say his say
Before he arrives to say it out.
It is under the small, dim, summer star.
I know not who these mute folk are
Who share the unlit place with me—
Those stones out under the low-limbed tree
Doubtless bear names that the mosses mar.
They are tireless folk, but slow and sad,
Though two, close-keeping, are lass and lad,—
With none among them that ever sings,
And yet, in view of how many things,
As sweet companions as might be had.

My November Guest

My sorrow, when she's here with me,
Thinks these dark days of autumn rain
Are beautiful as days can be;
She loves the bare, the withered tree;
She walks the sodden pasture lane.
Her pleasure will not let me stay.
She talks and I am fain to list:
She's glad the birds are gone away,
She's glad her simple worsted gray
Is silver now with clinging mist.
The desolate, deserted trees,
The faded earth, the heavy sky,
The beauties she so truly sees,
She thinks I have no eye for these,
And vexes me for reason why.
Not yesterday I learned to know
The love of bare November days
Before the coming of the snow,
But it were vain to tell her so,
And they are better for her praise.

Love and a Question

A stranger came to the door at eve,
And he spoke the bridegroom fair.
He bore a green-white stick in his hand,
And, for all burden, care.
He asked with the eyes more than the lips
For a shelter for the night,
And he turned and looked at the road afar
Without a window light.
The bridegroom came forth into the porch
With, 'Let us look at the sky,
And question what of the night to be,
Stranger, you and I.'
The woodbine leaves littered the yard,
The woodbine berries were blue,
Autumn, yes, winter was in the wind;
'Stranger, I wish I knew.'
Within, the bride in the dusk alone
Bent over the open fire,
Her face rose-red with the glowing coal
And the thought of the heart's desire.
The bridegroom looked at the weary road,
Yet saw but her within,
And wished her heart in a case of gold
And pinned with a silver pin.
The bridegroom thought it little to give
A dole of bread, a purse,
A heartfelt prayer for the poor of God,
Or for the rich a curse;
But whether or not a man was asked
To mar the love of two
By harboring woe in the bridal house,
The bridegroom wished he knew.

A Late Walk

When I go up through the mowing field,
The headless aftermath,
Smooth-laid like thatch with the heavy dew,
Half closes the garden path.
And when I come to the garden ground,
The whir of sober birds
Up from the tangle of withered weeds
Is sadder than any words.
A tree beside the wall stands bare,
But a leaf that lingered brown,
Disturbed, I doubt not, by my thought,
Comes softly rattling down.
I end not far from my going forth
By picking the faded blue
Of the last remaining aster flower
To carry again to you.

Stars

How countlessly they congregate
O'er our tumultuous snow,
Which flows in shapes as tall as trees
When wintry winds do blow!—
As if with keenness for our fate,
Our faltering few steps on
To white rest, and a place of rest
Invisible at dawn,—
And yet with neither love nor hate,
Those stars like some snow-white
Minerva's snow-white marble eyes
Without the gift of sight.

Storm Fear

When the wind works against us in the dark,
And pelts with snow
The lowest chamber window on the east,
And whispers with a sort of stifled bark,
The beast,
'Come out! Come out!'—
It costs no inward struggle not to go,
Ah, no!
I count our strength,
Two and a child,
Those of us not asleep subdued to mark
How the cold creeps as the fire dies at length,—
How drifts are piled,
Dooryard and road ungraded,
Till even the comforting barn grows far away
And my heart owns a doubt
Whether 'tis in us to arise with day
And save ourselves unaided.

Wind and Window Flower

Lovers, forget your love,
And list to the love of these,
She a window flower,
And he a winter breeze.
When the frosty window veil
Was melted down at noon,
And the cagèd yellow bird
Hung over her in tune,
He marked her through the pane,
He could not help but mark,
And only passed her by,
To come again at dark.
He was a winter wind,
Concerned with ice and snow,
Dead weeds and unmated birds,
And little of love could know.
But he sighed upon the sill,
He gave the sash a shake,
As witness all within
Who lay that night awake.
Perchance he half prevailed
To win her for the flight
From the firelit looking-glass
And warm stove-window light.
But the flower leaned aside
And thought of naught to say,
And morning found the breeze
A hundred miles away.

To the Thawing Wind (audio)

Come with rain, O loud Southwester!
Bring the singer, bring the nester;
Give the buried flower a dream;
Make the settled snow-bank steam;
Find the brown beneath the white;
But whate'er you do to-night,
Bathe my window, make it flow,
Melt it as the ices go;
Melt the glass and leave the sticks
Like a hermit's crucifix;
Burst into my narrow stall;
Swing the picture on the wall;
Run the rattling pages o'er;
Scatter poems on the floor;
Turn the poet out of door.

A Prayer in Spring

Oh, give us pleasure in the flowers to-day;
And give us not to think so far away
As the uncertain harvest; keep us here
All simply in the springing of the year.
Oh, give us pleasure in the orchard white,
Like nothing else by day, like ghosts by night;
And make us happy in the happy bees,
The swarm dilating round the perfect trees.
And make us happy in the darting bird
That suddenly above the bees is heard,
The meteor that thrusts in with needle bill,
And off a blossom in mid air stands still.
For this is love and nothing else is love,
The which it is reserved for God above
To sanctify to what far ends He will,
But which it only needs that we fulfil.

Flower-gathering

I left you in the morning,
And in the morning glow,
You walked a way beside me
To make me sad to go.
Do you know me in the gloaming,
Gaunt and dusty grey with roaming?
Are you dumb because you know me not,
Or dumb because you know?
All for me? And not a question
For the faded flowers gay
That could take me from beside you
For the ages of a day?
They are yours, and be the measure
Of their worth for you to treasure,
The measure of the little while
That I've been long away.

Rose Pogonias

A saturated meadow,
Sun-shaped and jewel-small,
A circle scarcely wider
Than the trees around were tall;
Where winds were quite excluded,
And the air was stifling sweet
With the breath of many flowers,—
A temple of the heat.
There we bowed us in the burning,
As the sun's right worship is,
To pick where none could miss them
A thousand orchises;
For though the grass was scattered,
Yet every second spear
Seemed tipped with wings of color,
That tinged the atmosphere.
We raised a simple prayer
Before we left the spot,
That in the general mowing
That place might be forgot;
Or if not all so favoured,
Obtain such grace of hours,
That none should mow the grass there
While so confused with flowers.

Asking for Roses

A house that lacks, seemingly, mistress and master,
With doors that none but the wind ever closes,
Its floor all littered with glass and with plaster;
It stands in a garden of old-fashioned roses.
I pass by that way in the gloaming with Mary;
'I wonder,' I say, 'who the owner of those is.
'Oh, no one you know,' she answers me airy,
'But one we must ask if we want any roses.'
So we must join hands in the dew coming coldly
There in the hush of the wood that reposes,
And turn and go up to the open door boldly,
And knock to the echoes as beggars for roses.
'Pray, are you within there, Mistress Who-were-you?'
'Tis Mary that speaks and our errand discloses.
'Pray, are you within there? Bestir you, bestir you!
'Tis summer again; there's two come for roses.
'A word with you, that of the singer recalling—
Old Herrick: a saying that every maid knows is
A flower unplucked is but left to the falling,
And nothing is gained by not gathering roses.'
We do not loosen our hands' intertwining
(Not caring so very much what she supposes),
There when she comes on us mistily shining
And grants us by silence the boon of her roses.

WAITING AFIELD AT DUSK

What things for dream there are when spectre-like,
Moving among tall haycocks lightly piled,
I enter alone upon the stubble field,
From which the laborers' voices late have died,
And in the antiphony of afterglow
And rising full moon, sit me down
Upon the full moon's side of the first haycock
And lose myself amid so many alike.
I dream upon the opposing lights of the hour,
Preventing shadow until the moon prevail;
I dream upon the night-hawks peopling heaven,
Each circling each with vague unearthly cry,
Or plunging headlong with fierce twang afar;
And on the bat's mute antics, who would seem
Dimly to have made out my secret place,
Only to lose it when he pirouettes,
And seek it endlessly with purblind haste;
On the last swallow's sweep; and on the rasp
In the abyss of odor and rustle at my back,
That, silenced by my advent, finds once more,
After an interval, his instrument,
And tries once—twice—and thrice if I be there;
And on the worn book of old-golden song
I brought not here to read, it seems, but hold
And freshen in this air of withering sweetness;
But on the memory of one absent most,
For whom these lines when they shall greet her eye.

In a Vale

When I was young, we dwelt in a vale
By a misty fen that rang all night,
And thus it was the maidens pale
I knew so well, whose garments trail
Across the reeds to a window light.
The fen had every kind of bloom,
And for every kind there was a face,
And a voice that has sounded in my room
Across the sill from the outer gloom.
Each came singly unto her place,
But all came every night with the mist;
And often they brought so much to say
Of things of moment to which, they wist,
One so lonely was fain to list,
That the stars were almost faded away
Before the last went, heavy with dew,
Back to the place from which she came—
Where the bird was before it flew,
Where the flower was before it grew,
Where bird and flower were one and the same.
And thus it is I know so well
Why the flower has odor, the bird has song.
You have only to ask me, and I can tell.
No, not vainly there did I dwell,
Nor vainly listen all the night long.

A Dream Pang

I had withdrawn in forest, and my song
Was swallowed up in leaves that blew alway;
And to the forest edge you came one day
(This was my dream) and looked and pondered long,
But did not enter, though the wish was strong:
You shook your pensive head as who should say,
'I dare not—too far in his footsteps stray—
He must seek me would he undo the wrong.
Not far, but near, I stood and saw it all
Behind low boughs the trees let down outside;
And the sweet pang it cost me not to call
And tell you that I saw does still abide.
But 'tis not true that thus I dwelt aloof,
For the wood wakes, and you are here for proof.

In Neglect

They leave us so to the way we took,
As two in whom they were proved mistaken,
That we sit sometimes in the wayside nook,
With mischievous, vagrant, seraphic look,
And try if we cannot feel forsaken.

The Vantage Point

If tired of trees I seek again mankind,
Well I know where to hie me—in the dawn,
To a slope where the cattle keep the lawn.
There amid lolling juniper reclined,
Myself unseen, I see in white defined
Far off the homes of men, and farther still,
The graves of men on an opposing hill,
Living or dead, whichever are to mind.
And if by moon I have too much of these,
I have but to turn on my arm, and lo,
The sun-burned hillside sets my face aglow,
My breathing shakes the bluet like a breeze,
I smell the earth, I smell the bruisèd plant,
I look into the crater of the ant.

Mowing

There was never a sound beside the wood but one,
And that was my long scythe whispering to the ground.
What was it it whispered? I knew not well myself;
Perhaps it was something about the heat of the sun,
Something, perhaps, about the lack of sound—
And that was why it whispered and did not speak.
It was no dream of the gift of idle hours,
Or easy gold at the hand of fay or elf:
Anything more than the truth would have seemed too weak
To the earnest love that laid the swale in rows,
Not without feeble-pointed spikes of flowers
(Pale orchises), and scared a bright green snake.
The fact is the sweetest dream that labor knows.
My long scythe whispered and left the hay to make.

Going for Water

The well was dry beside the door,
And so we went with pail and can
Across the fields behind the house
To seek the brook if still it ran;
Not loth to have excuse to go,
Because the autumn eve was fair
(Though chill), because the fields were ours,
And by the brook our woods were there.
We ran as if to meet the moon
That slowly dawned behind the trees,
The barren boughs without the leaves,
Without the birds, without the breeze.
But once within the wood, we paused
Like gnomes that hid us from the moon,
Ready to run to hiding new
With laughter when she found us soon.
Each laid on other a staying hand
To listen ere we dared to look,
And in the hush we joined to make
We heard, we knew we heard the brook.
A note as from a single place,
A slender tinkling fall that made
Now drops that floated on the pool
Like pearls, and now a silver blade.

PART II

Revelation

We make ourselves a place apart
Behind light words that tease and flout,
But oh, the agitated heart
Till someone find us really out.
'Tis pity if the case require
(Or so we say) that in the end
We speak the literal to inspire
The understanding of a friend.
But so with all, from babes that play
At hide-and-seek to God afar,
So all who hide too well away
Must speak and tell us where they are.

The Trial by Existence

Even the bravest that are slain
Shall not dissemble their surprise
On waking to find valor reign,
Even as on earth, in paradise;
And where they sought without the sword
Wide fields of asphodel fore'er,
To find that the utmost reward
Of daring should be still to dare.
The light of heaven falls whole and white
And is not shattered into dyes,
The light for ever is morning light;
The hills are verdured pasture-wise;
The angel hosts with freshness go,
And seek with laughter what to brave;—
And binding all is the hushed snow
Of the far-distant breaking wave.
And from a cliff-top is proclaimed
The gathering of the souls for birth,
The trial by existence named,
The obscuration upon earth.
And the slant spirits trooping by
In streams and cross- and counter-streams
Can but give ear to that sweet cry
For its suggestion of what dreams!
And the more loitering are turned
To view once more the sacrifice
Of those who for some good discerned
Will gladly give up paradise.
And a white shimmering concourse rolls
Toward the throne to witness there
The speeding of devoted souls
Which God makes his especial care.
And none are taken but who will,
Having first heard the life read out
That opens earthward, good and ill,
Beyond the shadow of a doubt;

And very beautifully God limns,
And tenderly, life's little dream,
But naught extenuates or dims,
Setting the thing that is supreme.
Nor is there wanting in the press
Some spirit to stand simply forth,
Heroic in its nakedness,
Against the uttermost of earth.
The tale of earth's unhonored things
Sounds nobler there than 'neath the sun;
And the mind whirls and the heart sings,
And a shout greets the daring one.
But always God speaks at the end:
'One thought in agony of strife
The bravest would have by for friend,
The memory that he chose the life;
But the pure fate to which you go
Admits no memory of choice,
Or the woe were not earthly woe
To which you give the assenting voice.'
And so the choice must be again,
But the last choice is still the same;
And the awe passes wonder then,
And a hush falls for all acclaim.
And God has taken a flower of gold
And broken it, and used therefrom
The mystic link to bind and hold
Spirit to matter till death come.
'Tis of the essence of life here,
Though we choose greatly, still to lack
The lasting memory at all clear,
That life has for us on the wrack
Nothing but what we somehow chose;
Thus are we wholly stripped of pride
In the pain that has but one close,
Bearing it crushed and mystified.

In Equal Sacrifice

Thus of old the Douglas did:
He left his land as he was bid
With the royal heart of Robert the Bruce
In a golden case with a golden lid,
To carry the same to the Holy Land;
By which we see and understand
That that was the place to carry a heart
At loyalty and love's command,
And that was the case to carry it in.
The Douglas had not far to win
Before he came to the land of Spain,
Where long a holy war had been
Against the too-victorious Moor;
And there his courage could not endure
Not to strike a blow for God
Before he made his errand sure.
And ever it was intended so,
That a man for God should strike a blow,
No matter the heart he has in charge
For the Holy Land where hearts should go.
But when in battle the foe were met,
The Douglas found him sore beset,
With only strength of the fighting arm
For one more battle passage yet—
And that as vain to save the day
As bring his body safe away—
Only a signal deed to do
And a last sounding word to say.
The heart he wore in a golden chain
He swung and flung forth into the plain,
And followed it crying 'Heart or death!'
And fighting over it perished fain.
So may another do of right,
Give a heart to the hopeless fight,
The more of right the more he loves;
So may another redouble might

For a few swift gleams of the angry brand,
Scorning greatly not to demand
In equal sacrifice with his
The heart he bore to the Holy Land.

THE TUFT OF FLOWERS

I went to turn the grass once after one
Who mowed it in the dew before the sun.
The dew was gone that made his blade so keen
Before I came to view the leveled scene.
I looked for him behind an isle of trees;
I listened for his whetstone on the breeze.
But he had gone his way, the grass all mown,
And I must be, as he had been,—alone,
'As all must be,' I said within my heart,
'Whether they work together or apart.'
But as I said it, swift there passed me by
On noiseless wing a 'wildered butterfly,
Seeking with memories grown dim o'er night
Some resting flower of yesterday's delight.
And once I marked his flight go round and round,
As where some flower lay withering on the ground.
And then he flew as far as eye could see,
And then on tremulous wing came back to me.
I thought of questions that have no reply,
And would have turned to toss the grass to dry;
But he turned first, and led my eye to look
At a tall tuft of flowers beside a brook,
A leaping tongue of bloom the scythe had spared
Beside a reedy brook the scythe had bared.
I left my place to know them by their name,
Finding them butterfly weed when I came.
The mower in the dew had loved them thus,
By leaving them to flourish, not for us,
Nor yet to draw one thought of ours to him.
But from sheer morning gladness at the brim.
The butterfly and I had lit upon,
Nevertheless, a message from the dawn,
That made me hear the wakening birds around,
And hear his long scythe whispering to the ground,
And feel a spirit kindred to my own;
So that henceforth I worked no more alone;

But glad with him, I worked as with his aid,
And weary, sought at noon with him the shade;
And dreaming, as it were, held brotherly speech
With one whose thought I had not hoped to reach.
'Men work together,' I told him from the heart,
'Whether they work together or apart.'

Spoils of the Dead

Two fairies it was
On a still summer day
Came forth in the woods
With the flowers to play.
The flowers they plucked
They cast on the ground
For others, and those
For still others they found.
Flower-guided it was
That they came as they ran
On something that lay
In the shape of a man.
The snow must have made
The feathery bed
When this one fell
On the sleep of the dead.
But the snow was gone
A long time ago,
And the body he wore
Nigh gone with the snow.
The fairies drew near
And keenly espied
A ring on his hand
And a chain at his side.
They knelt in the leaves
And eerily played
With the glittering things,
And were not afraid.
And when they went home
To hide in their burrow,
They took them along
To play with to-morrow.
When you came on death,
Did you not come flower-guided
Like the elves in the wood?
I remember that I did.

But I recognised death
With sorrow and dread,
And I hated and hate
The spoils of the dead.

Pan with Us

Pan came out of the woods one day,—
His skin and his hair and his eyes were gray,
The gray of the moss of walls were they,—
And stood in the sun and looked his fill
At wooded valley and wooded hill.
He stood in the zephyr, pipes in hand,
On a height of naked pasture land;
In all the country he did command
He saw no smoke and he saw no roof.
That was well! and he stamped a hoof.
His heart knew peace, for none came here
To this lean feeding save once a year
Someone to salt the half-wild steer,
Or homespun children with clicking pails
Who see no little they tell no tales.
He tossed his pipes, too hard to teach
A new-world song, far out of reach,
For a sylvan sign that the blue jay's screech
And the whimper of hawks beside the sun
Were music enough for him, for one.
Times were changed from what they were:
Such pipes kept less of power to stir
The fruited bough of the juniper
And the fragile bluets clustered there
Than the merest aimless breath of air.
They were pipes of pagan mirth,
And the world had found new terms of worth.
He laid him down on the sun-burned earth
And ravelled a flower and looked away—
Play? Play?—What should he play?

The Demiurge's Laugh

It was far in the sameness of the wood;
I was running with joy on the Demon's trail,
Though I knew what I hunted was no true god.
It was just as the light was beginning to fail
That I suddenly heard—all I needed to hear:
It has lasted me many and many a year.
The sound was behind me instead of before,
A sleepy sound, but mocking half,
As of one who utterly couldn't care.
The Demon arose from his wallow to laugh,
Brushing the dirt from his eye as he went;
And well I knew what the Demon meant.
I shall not forget how his laugh rang out.
I felt as a fool to have been so caught,
And checked my steps to make pretence
It was something among the leaves I sought
(Though doubtful whether he stayed to see).
Thereafter I sat me against a tree.

PART III

Now Close the Windows

Now close the windows and hush all the fields;
If the trees must, let them silently toss;
No bird is singing now, and if there is,
Be it my loss.
It will be long ere the marshes resume,
It will be long ere the earliest bird:
So close the windows and not hear the wind,
But see all wind-stirred.

A Line-storm Song

The line-storm clouds fly tattered and swift,
The road is forlorn all day,
Where a myriad snowy quartz stones lift,
And the hoof-prints vanish away.
The roadside flowers, too wet for the bee,
Expend their bloom in vain.
Come over the hills and far with me,
And be my love in the rain.

The birds have less to say for themselves
In the wood-world's torn despair
Than now these numberless years the elves,
Although they are no less there:
All song of the woods is crushed like some
Wild, easily shattered rose.
Come, be my love in the wet woods; come,
Where the boughs rain when it blows.

There is the gale to urge behind
And bruit our singing down,
And the shallow waters aflutter with wind
From which to gather your gown.
What matter if we go clear to the west,
And come not through dry-shod?
For wilding brooch shall wet your breast
The rain-fresh goldenrod.

Oh, never this whelming east wind swells
But it seems like the sea's return
To the ancient lands where it left the shells
Before the age of the fern;
And it seems like the time when after doubt
Our love came back amain.
Oh, come forth into the storm and rout
And be my love in the rain.

October

O hushed October morning mild,
Thy leaves have ripened to the fall;
To-morrow's wind, if it be wild,
Should waste them all.
The crows above the forest call;
To-morrow they may form and go.
O hushed October morning mild,
Begin the hours of this day slow,
Make the day seem to us less brief.
Hearts not averse to being beguiled,
Beguile us in the way you know;
Release one leaf at break of day;
At noon release another leaf;
One from our trees, one far away;
Retard the sun with gentle mist;
Enchant the land with amethyst.
Slow, slow!
For the grapes' sake, if they were all,
Whose leaves already are burnt with frost,
Whose clustered fruit must else be lost—
For the grapes' sake along the wall.

My Butterfly

Thine emulous fond flowers are dead, too,
And the daft sun-assaulter, he
That frighted thee so oft, is fled or dead:
Save only me
(Nor is it sad to thee!)
Save only me
There is none left to mourn thee in the fields.
The gray grass is not dappled with the snow;
Its two banks have not shut upon the river;
But it is long ago—
It seems forever—
Since first I saw thee glance,
With all the dazzling other ones,
In airy dalliance,
Precipitate in love,
Tossed, tangled, whirled and whirled above,
Like a limp rose-wreath in a fairy dance.
When that was, the soft mist
Of my regret hung not on all the land,
And I was glad for thee,
And glad for me, I wist.
Thou didst not know, who tottered, wandering on high,
That fate had made thee for the pleasure of the wind,
With those great careless wings,
Nor yet did I.
And there were other things:
It seemed God let thee flutter from his gentle clasp:
Then fearful he had let thee win
Too far beyond him to be gathered in,
Snatched thee, o'er eager, with ungentle grasp.
Ah! I remember me
How once conspiracy was rife
Against my life—
The languor of it and the dreaming fond;
Surging, the grasses dizzied me of thought,
The breeze three odors brought,

And a gem-flower waved in a wand!
Then when I was distraught
And could not speak,
Sidelong, full on my cheek,
What should that reckless zephyr fling
But the wild touch of thy dye-dusty wing!
I found that wing broken to-day!
For thou are dead, I said,
And the strange birds say.
I found it with the withered leaves
Under the eaves.

Reluctance

Out through the fields and the woods
And over the walls I have wended;
I have climbed the hills of view
And looked at the world, and descended;
I have come by the highway home,
And lo, it is ended.
The leaves are all dead on the ground,
Save those that the oak is keeping
To ravel them one by one
And let them go scraping and creeping
Out over the crusted snow,
When others are sleeping.
And the dead leaves lie huddled and still,
No longer blown hither and thither;
The last lone aster is gone;
The flowers of the witch-hazel wither;
The heart is still aching to seek,
But the feet question 'Whither?'
Ah, when to the heart of man
Was it ever less than a treason
To go with the drift of things,
To yield with a grace to reason,
And bow and accept and accept the end
Of a love or a season?

A NOTE ABOUT THE AUTHOR

Robert Frost (1874–1963) was an American poet. Born in San Francisco, Frost moved with his family to Lawrence, Massachusetts following the death of his father, a teacher and editor. There, he attended Lawrence High School and went on to study for a brief time at Dartmouth College before returning home to work as a teacher, factory worker, and newspaper delivery person. Certain of his calling as a poet, Frost sold his first poem in 1894, embarking on a career that would earn him acclaim and honor unlike any American poet before or since. Before his paternal grandfather's death, he purchased a farm in Derry, New Hampshire for Robert and his wife Elinor. For the next decade, Frost worked on the farm while writing poetry in the mornings before returning to teaching once more. In 1912, having moved to England, Frost published *A Boy's Will*, his first book of poems. Through the next several years, he wrote and published poetry while befriending such writers as Edward Thomas and Ezra Pound. In 1915, after publishing *North of Boston* (1914) in London, Frost returned to the United States to settle on another farm in Franconia, New Hampshire, where he continued writing and teaching and began lecturing. Over the next several decades, Frost published numerous collections of poems, including *New Hampshire: A Poem with Notes and Grace Notes* (1924) and *Collected Poems* (1931), winning a total of four Pulitzer Prizes and establishing his reputation as the foremost American poet of his generation.

A NOTE FROM THE PUBLISHER

Spanning many genres, from non-fiction essays to literature classics to children's books and lyric poetry, Mint Edition books showcase the master works of our time in a modern new package. The text is freshly typeset, is clean and easy to read, and features a new note about the author in each volume. Many books also include exclusive new introductory material. Every book boasts a striking new cover, which makes it as appropriate for collecting as it is for gift giving. Mint Edition books are only printed when a reader orders them, so natural resources are not wasted. We're proud that our books are never manufactured in excess and exist only in the exact quantity they need to be read and enjoyed.

bookfinity™

Discover more of your favorite classics with Bookfinity™.

- Track your reading with custom book lists.
- Get great book recommendations for your personalized Reader Type.
- Add reviews for your favorite books.
- AND MUCH MORE!

Visit **bookfinity.com** and take the fun Reader Type quiz to get started.

Enjoy our classic and modern companion pairings!

Classic & Modern

www.ingramcontent.com/pod-product-compliance
Lightning Source LLC
Chambersburg PA
CBHW020609030426
42337CB00013B/1282